# Made in

# Japan

By Reed Darmon

CHRONICLE BOOKS

SAN FRANCISCO

Page 254 constitutes a continuation
of the copyright page.

Library of Congress Cataloging-in-Publication
Data available.

ISBN-10: 0-8118-5073-0
ISBN-13: 978-0-8118-5073-5

Manufactured in China

Designed by Reed Darmon

Distributed in Canada by Raincoast Books
9050 Shaughnessy Street
Vancouver, British Columbia V6P 6E5

10 9 8 7 6 5 4 3 2 1

Chronicle Books LLC
85 Second Street
San Francisco, California 94105

www.chroniclebooks.com

This book is
dedicated to
Moto Hyun,
fellow traveler.

# Introduction

Japan's uniquely refined visual culture has long been a subject of
intense speculation, particularly among the Japanese, who with
justifiable pride have credited it variously to their poetic island
setting, four distinct seasons, national character set against
periods of isolationism, and (the far fringe theory) an extra gene.

From a Western perspective, it's tempting to seize upon an
aspect of Japanese culture and imagine that one has found a key
to unlocking its mysteries. The ancient Japanese religion of
Shinto, for instance, holds that sacred spirits exist in all things,
which would encourage a reverence for the physical, or the
material: the ancient tree, the graceful waterfall, the simple
teacup, the elegantly ergonomic tool. Does this love of the way

**Pages
from an
illustrated
book from
the 1870s.**

things look lead to the care in creating the perfect paper fan, or the aura of reverence accorded a perfume bottle in a magazine ad? Perhaps it accords with what philosopher Roland Barthes meant when he referred to Japan as the "empire of signs," the way a thing is often more than just a thing but is an archetype of itself. In this exuberant consumer culture, a paper fan can be at the same time a precious symbol of Japan and something to toss away.

Many elements of Japanese visual arts are inherited from China — cultural symbols, the calligraphic alphabet, a certain sense of formality. But, as with many ideas that come from outside, Japan imbued them with a sensuality, wit, and style. The game of baseball, for example, took on a more mannered and celebratory air when it took root in Japan, and the collectible baseball card became less about statistics and superstars and more about the art of play.

In the eighteenth century, the Japanese government levied consumption taxes in an attempt to restrict displays of wealth among the newly emerging middle class. These strictures forced craftsmen to lavish their skills on small private objects, like tiny ivory clasps or exquisite lacquer boxes. Did this tradition of great craftsmanship in detail and miniature formats lead to the Japanese flair for certain small-canvas genres of graphic art, like the matchbox or the postcard, both of which became rich showcases for the latest in design and social trends?

Modern commercial art grew directly from the traditions of the great Japanese woodblock-print industry of previous centuries, with its black outlined fields of color and smart, stylized compositions. It is interesting that when these Japanese prints arrived in Europe, they became great sources of inspiration to Western designers, helping to create art nouveau and art deco, so it's only natural that when Japanese artists saw these Western trends, they mastered them with ease.

By the beginning of the twentieth century in Japan, there was already a long tradition of small storybooks that mingled text and illustration on the same page. These picture books, or *manga*, prefigure and lead directly to the country's massive comic-book industry today. It's easy to imagine the geisha and samurai characters in these intricate picture books mutating over time into

**Pages from a comic book from the 1950s.**

the schoolgirl vixens and transforming robots of the present era. But there are many more threads to follow through popular culture hinted at by Japan's past. There is the love of detail and perfectionism, which leads to a love of miniaturization. Does this bring us to an actor in a rubber monster suit demolishing an exquisitely crafted model of Tokyo? There is the long tradition of dolls and puppets running alongside the fascination with mechanisms and automatons, which perhaps explains the ingenious, cheap children's toys of the early part of the century and the clever electronic devices of the later part. Has the love of the doll, the cartoon character, and the miniature come together in the Japanese love for the exceedingly cute, which has also become a motif in self-examining, experimental Japanese art?

Unique in Asia, Japan has had an urban middle class since the early twentieth century, with consumers shopping in a sophisticated marketplace. Commercial culture has become particularly urbane and self-aware, and the products that compete for customers, attention, and affection have enjoyed a storied evolution and history. This makes any attempt to assemble a sweeping review of this era of Japanese pop-cultural design a dizzying project. Japan's mastery of certain visual techniques — like multilayered and hidden humor, faux-naif draftsmanship, and a curious dry surrealism — is also a challenge for non-natives to understand.

Obviously, this can only be an idiosyncratic and personal ramble through a field that stretches endlessly in all directions. I offer this book as an entertainment, in respectful appreciation of the genius of Japanese popular design.

— Reed Darmon

**ABOVE:** This woodblock print, entitled "Children's Scenes – Zoo," was printed by Niuemon Akiyama in 1888 and shows a curious transitional phase in children's clothing styles.

**RIGHT:** A fashionable woman displays her modernity in the form of glasses and a ring in this woodblock print from the series "True Beauties," by Toyohara Chikanobu, 1898.

廟參拜記念
大廟大々神宮御参拝記念

徵古館

燒山院ケ山ロープ

外宮

山田電車線路

昭和四年十二月三日出版仝月十日印刷　宇治山田市岩渕町六九番地　發行人　山下宗兵衛

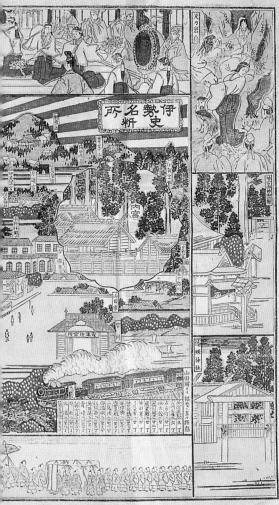

A woodblock print, a souvenir of a trip to Ise Shrine, the most sacred location of the Shinto religion. The print shows "must-see historical sites," scenes from religious ceremonies, and train connections.

**ABOVE:** Woodblock printed cards from a popular game called A Hundred Poems by a Hundred Poets in which the players try to match the poems and the images of famous twelfth-century poets.

**RIGHT:** A children's game called *menko* – which was played by throwing down little cards, aiming to hit and therefore win opponents' cards – is shown in this woodblock print from the end of the nineteenth century.

**RIGHT:** The Meiji Emperor (1867 to 1912) poses in this 6-foot-tall scroll below a poem attributed to him. The poem pays tribute to those who died during the conflicts of 1868 - 69 that brought about the modern era of government in Japan.

**LEFT:** The ancient Chinese characters "long-lasting and eternal" are used to describe this turn-of-the-century aerial view of the Imperial Palace in Tokyo, a detail from a chromolithograph mounted as a scroll.

This unattributed photograph, entitled
"Workman's Holiday," was taken by a Japanese
photographer and compiled for the West in a
book called *Japan, Described and Illustrated
by the Japanese*, 1898.

**Studio card photos
of gentlemen showing
the introduction of
Western-style clothing.**

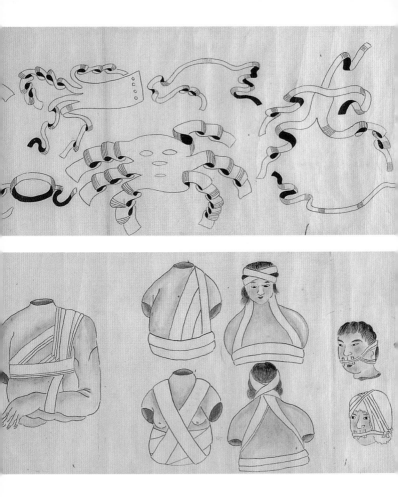

**Two sections of a long scroll illustrating bandaging techniques, hand drawn on rice paper, artist and date unknown.**

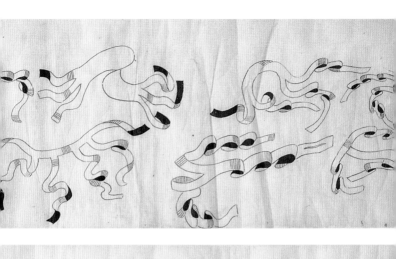

**ABOVE: An advertisement for Sunrise Brand Toothpaste, made by Nagaoka, Kyoto.**

**LEFT: A box of Lion Brand Sanitary Dentifrice, made by T. Kobayashi and Co.**

**RIGHT: Pieces of paper stating the virtues of various products of the Shounkan Matsumoto Pharmacy are spread from a hot-air balloon in this ad from around 1910.**

ハ月代

24

**ABOVE:** An art nouveau-style gift certificate for the Komatsu Store, Osaka.

**RIGHT:** A stylish package of hairpins.

**LEFT:** The calligraphy says "eternal," in honor of the imperial reign, on this ad for Imperial Succession Memorial Cigarettes.

FILATURES PREPARED
BY
TAISHOKAN

那伊下州信　本日大

大正館器械製絲

MADE IN JAPAN

RAW SILK
IIJIMASEISHI LTD.
TURTLE

飯島製絲株式會社

MADE IN JAPAN

RAW SILK

THE KAKUJU RAW SILK FILATURE LTD.
SIBATA FACTORY

鶴嘉製絲株式會社新發田工場

新潟縣新發田町

MADE IN JAPAN

"GOLD CANDLE"
SPECIAL REELING

13/15

SPRING

TRADE          MARK

GUNZE RAW SILK MFG. CO.
AYABE, KYOTO, JAPAN.

MADE IN JAPAN

**LEFT** and **RIGHT**:
Labels on bolts of
silk destined for
foreign markets.

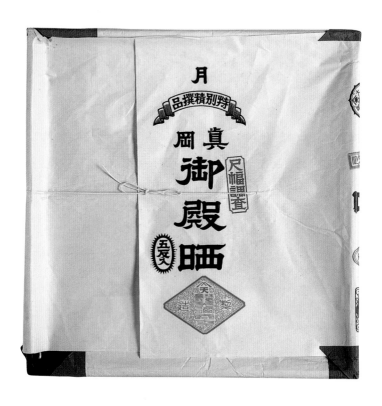

A lacquer serving tray that is "Specially and
carefully made" by the Maoka family company, still in its
original packaging from the first half of the century.

**A** woven straw covering helps to keep this bottle
of **O**zeki brand sake cool. *Ozeki* means "top sumo
wrestler," and this packaging is covered with
design elements relating to the sport.

The extremely stylized and moody masks of Noh theater,
which dates back to the fourteenth century, have become
popular decorative objects in their own right. Pictured here
are the maiden, Ko-omote, and Ko-Joyo, the old man.

Usobuki, or the "whistler," left, and Karsu-Tengu, the crow goblin, right, are affordable papier-mâché masks of characters in a style of theater called Kyogen, which originated as comic relief between acts in Noh theater.

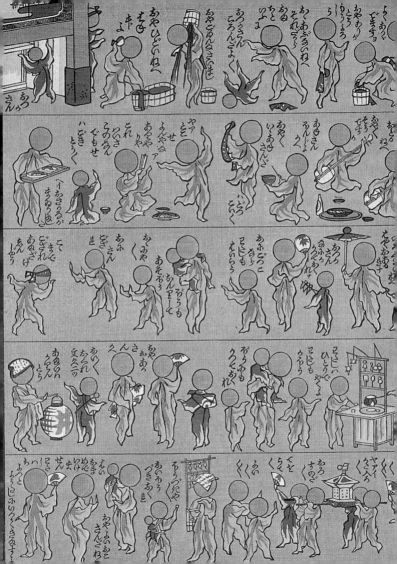

**ABOVE:** Souvenir prints from a Shinto temple dedicated to the fertility goddess, Inari. The mischievous fox spirit shown here is identified with Inari temples.

**LEFT:** A woodblock print by the artist Yoshifuji Utagawa (1828 - 87) seems to illustrate song lyrics about the events of the seasons; events include laundry day, the sale of *monjayaki* pancakes, parties, and religious ceremonies, all acted out by leaf people.

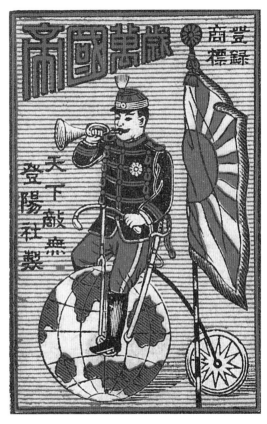

**ABOVE**: "Teikoku Banzai!" or "Long Live the Empire," reads the title on this matchbox cover.

**LEFT**: A saluting beauty in full parade attire on an unmarked photo postcard.

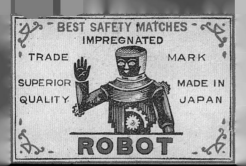

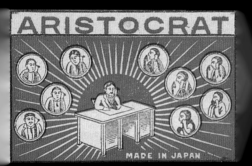

SAFETY MATCHES
MADE IN JAPAN.

仰天廣茂

SAFETY MATCHES

神戸石井米谷製造

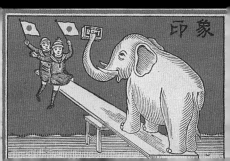

象印

Fantastic images of air travel on matchbox covers from the 1920s.

**A folding fan depicting the little-known heroes of early Japanese aviation.**

Votive cards, called *senjafuda*, which were
traditionally glued to temple doors, evolved over
time into collectible pieces of fine printing.
Here they advertise famous Kabuki theater stories,
above, and celebrated Kabuki actors, right.

あるかなきかのみくるそ

滑稽新聞社發行

At the beginning of the twentieth century a series of
sophisticated and finely printed postcards began to be
published in a series entitled *Ehagaki sekai,* or "World of
Picture Postcards," by the Humor Newspaper Company.
These cards were often amusing and filled with innuendos
and puns. Publication was shut down by 1907.

ABOVE: "One body, inseparable relationship" says this
postcard, with its charming metaphor for marriage. The
red thread symbolizes the relationship of couples.

LEFT: "Looking for ear wax, which can be elusive."

間一髪

滑稽新聞社發行

滑稽新聞社發行

ABOVE: A fishing mishap.

LEFT: The upper postcard is entitled "By the Skin of One's Teeth," and the lower card has no caption.

**ABOVE: A** backstage view reveals the trick behind the illusion of rolling waves in Kabuki theater stagecraft.

**LEFT: A** woman fastens her footwear in an indelicate manner.

ABOVE: A hand-tinted genre photo of
two Buddhist priests from the studios
of the commercial photographer
Kozaburo Tamamura.

RIGHT: A portion of a wall scroll from
around 1900 showing Kobo Daishi, the ninth-
century founder of the Shingon Buddhist
sect, surrounded by figures representing
various aspects of Buddhist teachings.

**A** pair of monk's
shoes made from
sections of
large bamboo.

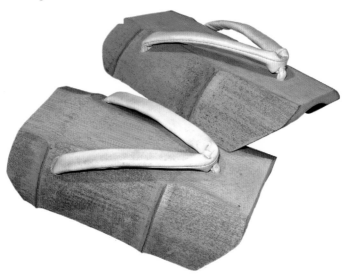

Paper charms collected during temple visits,
featuring, left to right, the early Buddhist priest
Kobo Daishi; Izuru Gongen, the fire protector;
and the Buddhist deity Fudou Myoo.

**LEFT:** The Sun Goddess, the principal deity of the ancient Shinto religion, emerges from the Heavenly Cave in this detail from a woodblock print by Yeitaku.

**RIGHT:** The Sun Goddess appears, in this scroll from the 1930s, among symbols that evoke Shinto's roots in agrarian culture and the cycles of nature.

Logos from a post-
card company and a
silk exporter, above,
and a character
advertising Pure
White rice cakes,
made in Kyoto, left.

**Bunriko Medicine:** "A powerful remedy for children's headpox, syphilis and rheumatism, etc."

**Zutsūru** headache medicine, made by Kajiura Kagaku Kenkyu jo; "Please take one immediately."

RIGHT: A package of Massage Plaster by the Okudo Medicine Company, showing plasters labeled with maladies such as toothache, stiff shoulders, sprain, backache, rheumatism, cuts, swelling, and burns.

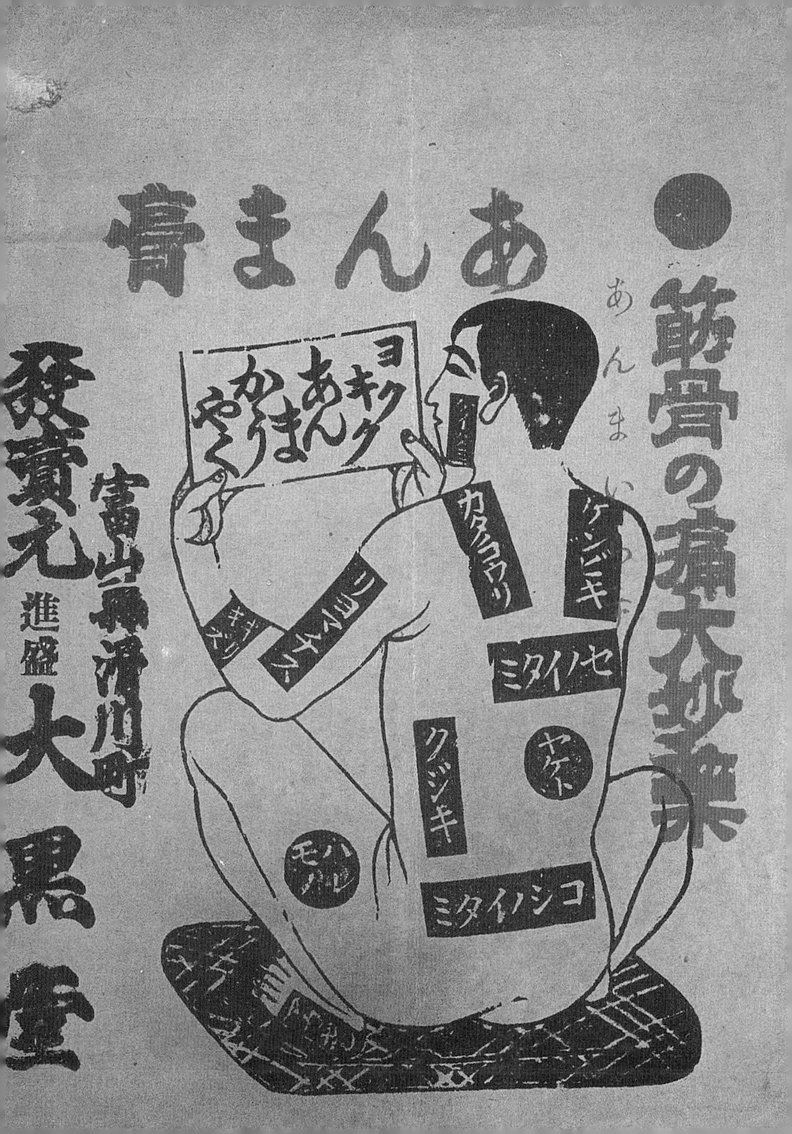

あんま膏
●筋骨の痛大妙薬
ヨクキク
あんま
かうやく
カタコウリ
ケンビキ
リヨウテ
セノイタミ
クジンキ
ヤケド
ハレモノ
コシノイタミ
發賣元
富山縣滑川町
進盛
大黒屋

RIGHT: No more stomach pain after you take this single-use digestive medicine from the Taishin Pharmaceutical Company.

A packet of Kaicho, or Top Condition Bowels stomachache and diarrhea medicine, and one of Rocket headache and fever medicine, both by Daiichi Pharmaceutical Company.

60   **Kainetsu san, "antifever and antipyretic" powder medicine.**

Santonin
Vermifuge
Pills.

A vial of
Santen Cough
Medicine.

A label for
Acrobatic Brand
tabi socks
(a type of cotton
footwear worn
with kimonos or by
those, like con-
struction workers
and performers,
who require
nonslip footwear).

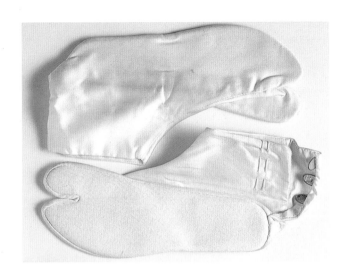

**ABOVE:** **A** pair of tabi socks, made of fine cotton for wearing in the home, and its package. The socks were made by **D**aimaru, **K**yoto.

**RIGHT:** **A** page from the magazine *Housewife's Friend* recommended cold weather items to make as gifts for the armed forces, including ear covers, silk underpants, knit wool socks, and warm vests with red pepper insect repellent.

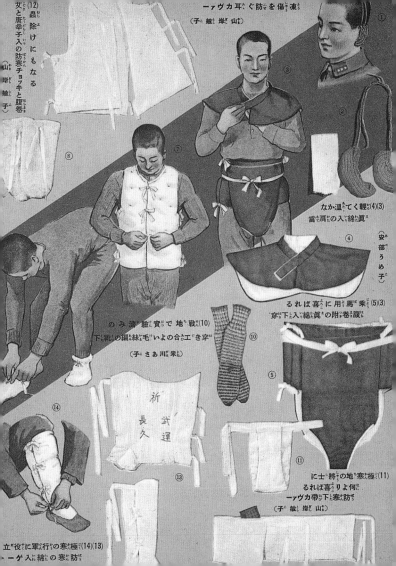

①

② なか温くて輕い(4)(3)
眞綿入の肩當

（安部ろめ子）

④ 乘馬用に喜ばれる(5)(3)
腹巻附の眞綿入下穿

凍傷を防ぐ耳ヴァカー
（山岸敏子）

(12)
蟲除けにもなる
防寒チョッキと腹巻
（山岸敏子）

実戰地で實驗済みの
毛いとの編靴下の工合穿
（米川あさ子）

極寒地将に士に(11)
何よりも喜ばれる
防寒下帯ヴァカー
（山岸敏子）

極寒行軍に役立(14)(13)
防寒綿入ケー

A poster from the Industrial Welfare Association
declaring that "The most important thing is getting
peaceful sleep," 1932.

A poster from the Industrial Welfare Association
that reads, "A serene sunrise. Take a deep breath," 1933.

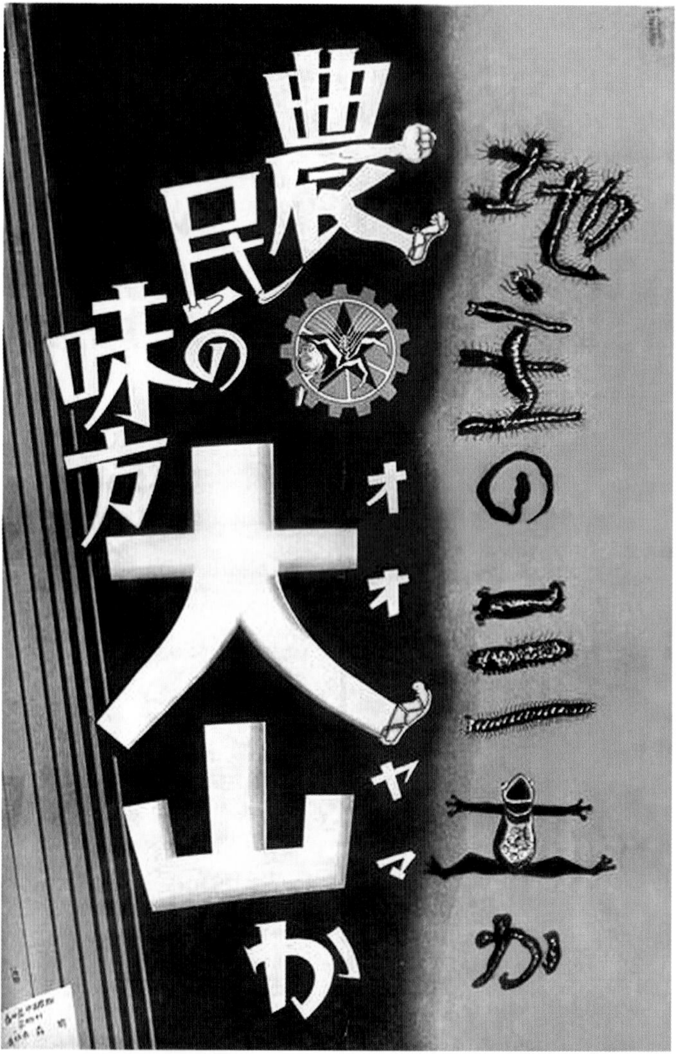

地主の三上か
農民の味方
大山か
オオヤマ

ABOVE: "Don't think of it as just a spark, but the mother of fires. Don't throw it out, extinguish it" reads a poster from the Industrial Welfare Association, 1932.

LEFT: "Mitsuchi, the Landowner, or Oyama, the Farmers' Friend?" asks an election campaign poster from 1928, with calligraphy formed from arms and legs on one side and vermin and a frog on the other.

**ABOVE:** An ad showing a modern cityscape as an achievement of the Asano Cement Company.

**RIGHT:** A ship laden with Japanese exports celebrates the Yokkaichi Expo on this New Year's postcard, 1936.

An advertisement for Miyako Dye by the Katsuraya Company, which states: "For the home and for tie-dyeing. Please be careful about imitations."

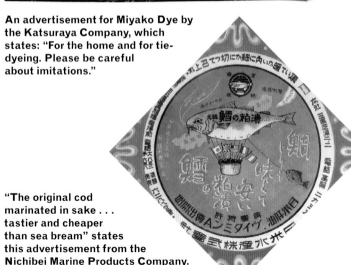

"The original cod marinated in sake . . . tastier and cheaper than sea bream" states this advertisement from the Nichibei Marine Products Company.

A box of Cocksec brand mosquito spirals made by Ueyamayei's Japan Insecticide Manufacturing Co.

Charcoal was common in everyday life through midcentury. Here is a box of Paulownia Ash, patented formula charcoal sticks for use in hand warmers.

RIGHT: An ad, designed by Sugiura Hisui in 1930, for Minori Cigarettes.

LEFT and BELOW: Early brands of cigarettes in the ten-per-pack size.

The beauties of spring in a fine commercial offset-printed poster for the
M. Furuya Company, purveyors of Japanese merchandise to the United States.

**ABOVE:** An ad for Hōshi Araiko Toilet Washing Powder.

**RIGHT:** A traditional beauty on a poster for White Crane Quality Sake, "made of the finest rice."

銘酒

白鶴

**RIGHT**: "Happiness and Long Life" states this gift box from Shoyeido and Co.

**BELOW**: Stylish design on a bag from Sogo Department Store, 1920s.

また匂ひ味には資生堂独特の
新鮮な趣きをもって居ります

**The Shiseido Cosmetics Company was a
pioneer in high-style advertising in the 1920s
and 1930s. Above, an advertisement for
tooth powder by an unknown artist;
above right, a newspaper ad for a Shiseido
fragrance, designed by Ayao Yamana in
1937; and right, an ad for Endermine liquid
face powder, by Yabe Sue, 1925.**

過酸化水素粉歯磨

たね兼かを水する粧しやう化け

粉う白じい無なの類るい

# 白色美顔水

三滴…一二分で

▲目の覺めるやうな

お化粧が出來…

▲生地迄美しくする

類の無い白粉…

アレ止に一等の……

美顔クリーム

**LEFT**: An ad for Beautiful White Face Water, "the face powder that also works as a lotion."

**BELOW**: A magazine ad for Reeto Compressed Face Powder that wishes customers "Good fortune in the New Year" and says this product will "become part of your skin, improve how your makeup looks and will make you feel enlivened."

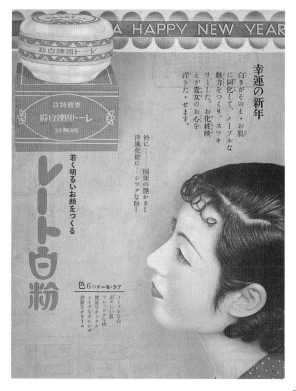

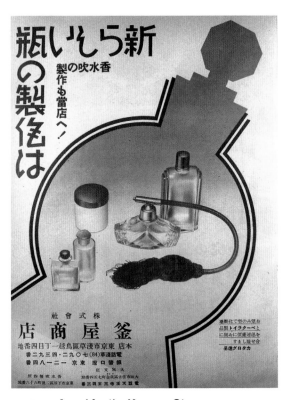

新らしい香水吹の製作も當店へ！
瓶の製作は

株式會社
釜屋商店
本店 東京市淺草區鳥越一丁目四番地
電話淺草(84)七〇九二・四三九二番
振替口座 東京 一二一八四番
大阪支店
大阪市住吉區宝來金五丁目四番地
香水吹製作所
東京市豊區下谷二町六十八番地

お望みの型で化粧品
ベークライト製品
と價廉運送に開かに
食せ放まし
カタログ進呈

**ABOVE:** An ad for the Kamaya Store, supplier of cosmetics bottles, perfume atomizers, and Bakelite products.

**RIGHT:** A poster for Housewife's Friend Company *yukata* fabric, 1930. A *yukata* is a summer or after-bath kimono usually made of light cotton.

84

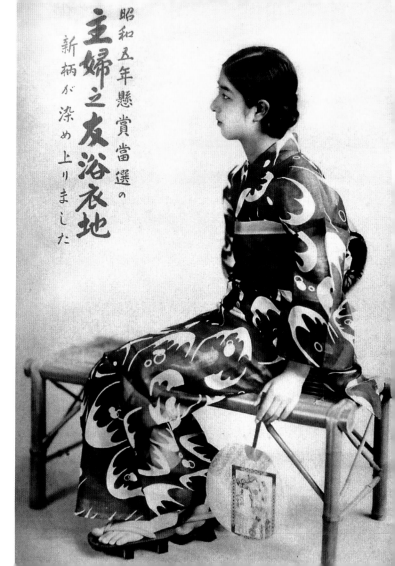

昭和五年懸賞當選の

主婦之友浴衣地

新柄が染め上りました

# ビタオール

## 整髪料

青函ビタオール
紫函ビタオール
ビタオールポマード液体
ビタオール練－ポマード

VITA-OL Hair Pomade

**ABOVE:** An ad for Hontzubaki brand Toniku Pomado (a phonetic spelling of tonic pomade) by Miyake-zo.

**RIGHT:** Styles of men's sweaters, from a magazine for knitting hobbyists.

**ABOVE:** Two visions of women, traditional and modern, on wall calendars, from 1937, left, and from 1941, right.

**RIGHT:** An ad for Misono Cream for Loving Skin, from the early 1930s, shows the famous actress Takiko Mizunoe (seated), who specialized in playing men's roles in the Shochiku Performing Company.

RIGHT: A package for a bolt of First Wave *yukata* fabric, a cotton used for making light kimonos.

ABOVE: The cover of a collection of romantic stories called *Fan Dance,* edited by Mikihiko Nakata, with a woodblock print on the cover by the modernist artist Yumeji (1884 - 1934).

RIGHT: A book entitled *Ceremonial Addresses and Speeches for the Current Era,* edited by the Oratory Study Group.

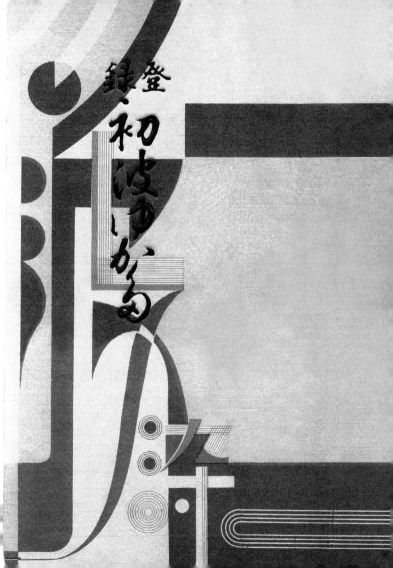

モダン
室町の陶酔郷

電日本橋 1078

In the 1920s and 1930s, the humble matchbox cover began to be a major form of advertising, and perhaps because of its ephemeral nature, a playground of modernist design.

LEFT: A matchbox advertising the Modern Euphoria Palace, a shop in the Muromachi area.

RIGHT: A matchbox advertising the Pure (nonalcohol) Coffee Shop, located on the lively Meiji University Street.

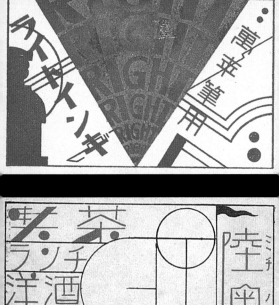

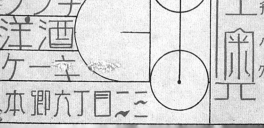

**ABOVE:** A matchbox ad for Koshien Bar in Osaka, left, and for Kokuyo Coffee and Western (or alcoholic) Beverages, right.

**LEFT:** A matchbox ad for Right Ink Company, "for fountain pens," top, and Michinoku Coffee and Tea shop selling cakes and Western alcoholic beverages, bottom.

A matchbox ad for *Ghost Stories: The Scary Castle*, "the ultimate in the macabre grotesque to give you a chill, playing at the Cinema Club, starting on the twentieth of this month."

An ad for Wings Coffee Shop near Shiba Shinmyo Keidai Shrine, left. Below left, a matchbox celebrating the Tokyo Imperial Flight Association. It says "Crossing the Pacific. Nonstop flight. Support our troops."

RIGHT: An idealized silhouette for men on an advertisement for the Tachibanaya Western Clothing Shop.

返品返金自由

# 店品洋屋花立

番四一三(5)湊電・隣上舘楽聚川湊

製チツマ進日　五沢上戸神

102

# ハネムーンホテル

横濱石川町大丸谷
電話②六一七八

A series of postcards from 1924, by Calpis Inc.,
makers of a popular milk beverage, shows the winners
of a design competition displaying the company's
products. The images here are "A Glass of Calpis by
the Window," left, and "Globe and Funnel" above.

クッニクビ

A pair of post-cards showing an elegant four-some in Western and Japanese dress, entitled "Picnic," from the Shiseido Cosmetics Company.

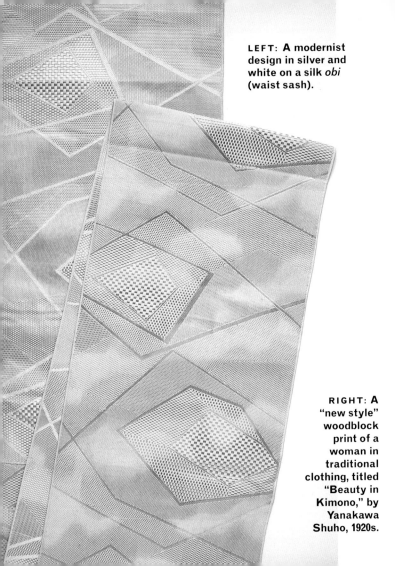

**LEFT: A** modernist design in silver and white on a silk *obi* (waist sash).

**RIGHT: A** "new style" woodblock print of a woman in traditional clothing, titled "Beauty in Kimono," by Yanakawa Shuho, 1920s.

109

The Japanese government's monopoly on cigarette production and sales from 1904 to 1985 allowed for the sophisticated package designs and serene brand names of the period, including **D**awn cigarettes, above, and **L**ight cigarettes, right.

ABOVE: Words are stacked like architecture on this
card announcing the Japan World Expo, held on the
2,600th anniversary of the Japanese nation, 1940.

RIGHT: A flyer announcing the first-ever national census on
October 10, 1921, encouraging people to report their names,
family statistics, birthdays, birthplaces, and occupations.

**ABOVE:** A labor union poster from the 1940s, which states: "Japanese National Railroad workers take the lead of all workers in staging a general strike!"

**RIGHT:** A poster designed by Masamu Yanase in 1935, announcing the Fourteenth National Convention of the National Farmers' Union.

全国農民組合第十四回全国大会

一九三五年 四月 廿八日

於大阪 天六市民会舘

全農を守れ 強くらろ！

全国土地作料を引下げさせ
生活向上をさせろ
労びか者と共に戦ふ

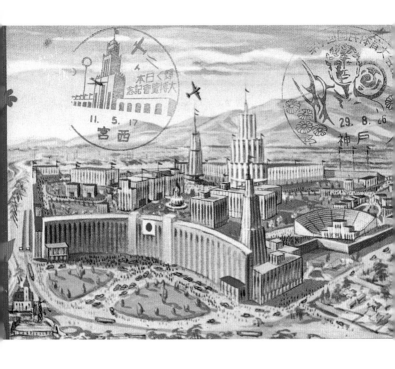

ABOVE: A postcard souvenir of the Commemoration of Glorious Japan Exposition of 1942.

RIGHT: A postcard celebrating the Exposition of the Peace of the Pan Pacific, Nagoya, 1937. Printed by the Nagoya Printing Company.

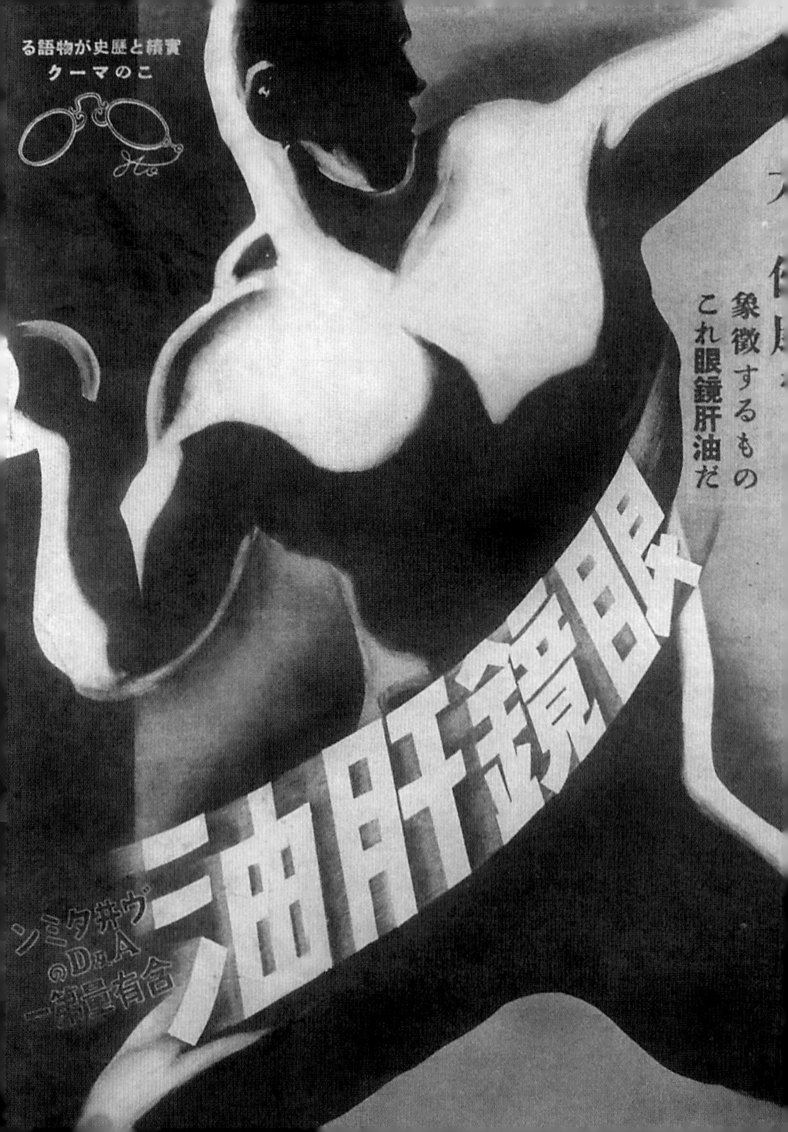

實績と歴史が物語る
このマーク
象徴するもの
これ眼鏡肝油だ
眼鏡肝油
ヴ井タミンA.Dの含有量第一

ABOVE: A magazine ad for Kisooru Liquid Plaster promises to help athletes recover from pain and fatigue.

LEFT: Magazine ad for products of the Sentaro Store, Osaka, announces "The highest amounts of vitamins A and D" are contained in Eyeglass Brand Liver Oil.

冬の用品

WINTER SPORTS

ABOVE and RIGHT: Flyers celebrating winter sports
while advertising the Mizuno Sporting Goods
Company, 1930s. The illustrations are signed "Iwao."

**ABOVE:** A magazine review of the Olympics of 1936, published by the Japan Sports Association.

**LEFT:** "[Go to] Hamadera" suggests this poster for a well-known park in Osaka, famous for its pine grove and swimming pool. The illustration is by R. Takeoka.

**A** girl in **C**hinese dress holding a flag representing the various ethnicities of **C**hina is greeted by a girl from **J**apan in this postcard from the 1930s.

This postcard, which says "10 Billion"
(presumably the number of yen needed for the
war effort), was painted by the Paris-trained
artist Leonard Tsuguharu Foujita.

賀正

堅期持久
長期建設

元旦

S.co

**ABOVE:** Every aspect of life was altered during
the war years, even this postcard expressing best
wishes for the new year.

**RIGHT:** "Soldiers on the battlefield need bullets and
food" declares this flyer promoting government bonds
for sale at the post office by the Finance Ministry, 1937.

戦線の将兵に
弾丸を！
糧食を！

四月廿二日ヨリ五月三日マデ
郵便局賣出し
支那事變國債

127

**ABOVE:** This postcard reminds citizens to "Look after wounded soldiers who protected the country."

**RIGHT:** A card announcing the services of the post office, including postal savings, deposits, and remittances.

振替貯金

取引ニ
送金ニ

A poster celebrating travel by train, from the Japanese Government Railways, 1938.

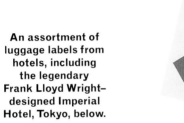

An assortment of luggage labels from hotels, including the legendary Frank Lloyd Wright–designed Imperial Hotel, Tokyo, below.

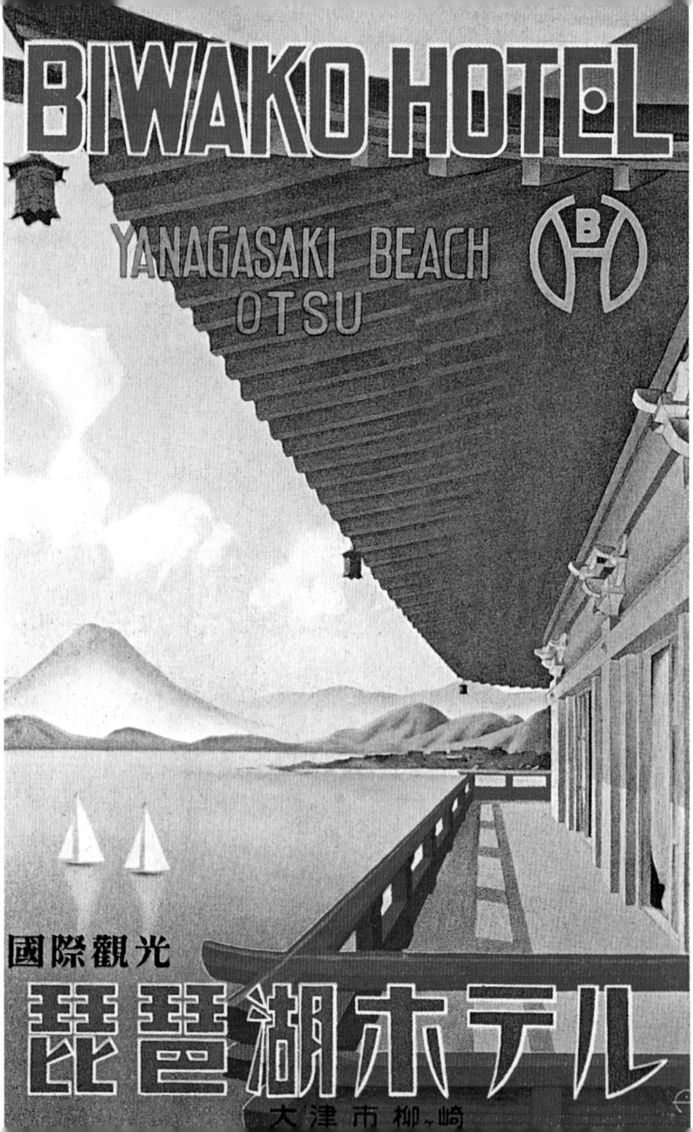

BIWAKO HOTEL
YANAGASAKI BEACH
OTSU
國際觀光
琵琶湖ホテル
大津市柳ヶ崎

ABOVE: A diagram of the first-class view room
on the Osaka Shosen Kaisha ocean liner the *Kogana*.

LEFT: A flyer for the Biwako Hotel, Yanagasaki Beach, Otsu.

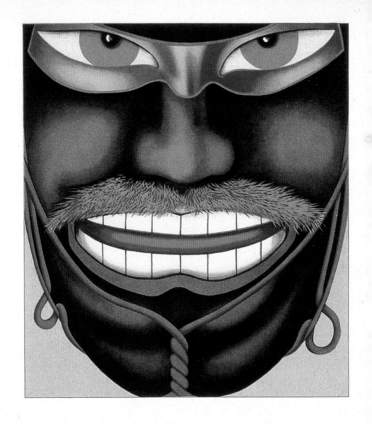

のみのコバタ

# カモス魔歯

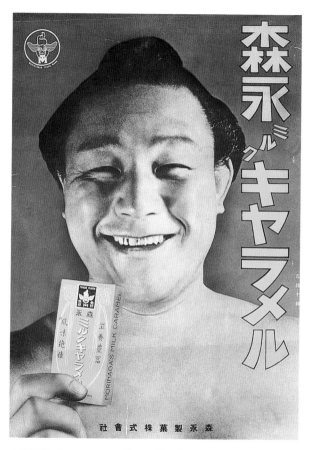

ABOVE: A sumo wrestler smiles in an ad for
Morinaga's Milk Caramel from the 1930s.

LEFT: Brilliant white teeth smile through
a samurai mask in this ad for Sumoka
Toothpaste for Smokers, 1933.

全日本最高標準品
ユアサ蓄電池

小倉石油給油所

タクシーの御用命は是非
安くまる
よい車で 阪神バス
タクシー部へ
HANSHIN BUS TAXI

| 営業所電話 | 西宮1701 (東口) | 芦屋2449 (芦屋) | 尼崎393 (尼崎) |
|---|---|---|---|
| | 西宮1026 (香ヶ尾) | 御影3518 (六甲道) | 尼崎185 (出屋敷) |
| | 宮宮281 (鳴尾) | 御影3518 (現在家) | 尼崎1265 (神崎) |
| | 西宮468 (甲子園) | 呉合959 (神戸) | 伊丹4 (伊丹) |

138

ABOVE: A matchbook cover advertising the
Restaurant Ichibawa. The words in the middle of
the road make up the name of a national highway,
suggesting that the restaurant is a highway diner.

LEFT: Matchbook covers advertising, from top
to bottom, Yuasa Car Batteries, Ogura Oil Gas
Station (a predecessor of Nippon Oil Corporation),
and the services of Hanshin Bus Taxi.

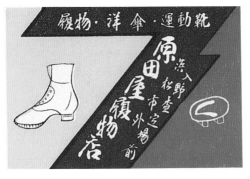

Matchboxes
advertising
footwear
from the
Haradaya
Shoes Shop,
Leaders Shoes,
and the Seki
Store.

清野理髪舘

日進堂理髪舘
巌松堂書店筋向横丁

小山 4の21
第2朝日湯東

Barber shops and hair
care products display
a very Western style
in these matchbox
covers for the Kiyono
Barber Shop, top left,
the Nisshindo Barber
Shop, top right,
and an ad for Hair
Growth Tonic, bottom.

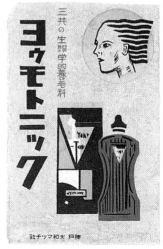

**ABOVE**: Lunches are commonly delivered to shops and homes in boxes called *bento*. These matchboxes are advertising the services of the Shore Chief, left, and Everybody's Restaurant, specializing in buckwheat noodles, right.

**RIGHT**: A casual 1950s brushwork style in an ad for the Osanai Western Clothing Store.

洋品

既製服

資生堂チエイン

オサナイ洋品店

ABOVE: "It soaks through my skin," says an ad for Beautiful Club Body Cream.

RIGHT: Ads from women's magazines, clockwise from top left: Reeto Face Powder, Penin Cream Pomade, Ekiserin Wool Detergent, and Utena Cosmetics.

Lithographed fans
portraying standards
of beauty in the
1940s for women in
traditional and
modern dress.

147

# 平凡

歌と映画の娯楽雑誌

平凡第六巻第二號 毎月一回五日發行 昭和二十五年二月一日印刷 昭和二十五年四月十日 第三種郵便物認可 昭和二十九年二月五日發行

原 節子

松竹
**想ひ出のボレロ**
大林清

特集
歌の明星大いに語る

松竹歌劇スタア花形くらべ

2

**LEFT**: The famous actress Setsuko Hara on the cover of the entertainment magazine *Heibon*, 1950.

**ABOVE**: An issue of the humor and entertainment magazine *Shodan*, 1942.

**LEFT**: A magazine called *Fujin Kurabu,* or "Women's Club," April 1936.

Early evolution of dewy-eyed cuteness.
LEFT: A postcard by an unknown artist.
BELOW: The cover of a comic book series called "Mom,
Can You Hear Me?" the story of adopted children, 1960.

**ABOVE:** Action comics for boys, clockwise from upper left, *Kenpo the Ronin, Wind Boy, Mysterious Land of Gold,* and *Cheering for Ganta.*

**RIGHT:** A cover of *Shonen Gaho,* or "Boy Illustrated." The hero, Tsukikage Shiro, is dressed in a standard student uniform.

# 月影四郎

## 風雪の巻

少年画報 第八巻 新年号・ふろく 第一号

田野武

**ABOVE**: **A** comic book, entitled *Anmitsu Komachi*, or "Sweet Cake Girl," tells the adventures of a partly independent, partly traditional girl, 1950s.

**RIGHT**: **A** magazine for young people called *Childhood Club*, 1940s.

幼年倶樂部第十六卷第八號　昭和十四年八月一日發行　昭和十年七月十日第三種郵便物認可（毎月一回一日發行）大正十四年二月二十八日第二種郵便物認可

# 幼年倶樂部

## 臣道實踐　職域奉公

## 八月號

ヤマモトサンノ
　マエニ
ナカムラサン、ガ
　　イマス。
サトーサンノ
　ウシロニ
タナカサンガ
　　イマス。

ナンニモ
アリマセン。

上

上

三十一

156

Two books of language and speech studies for the early grades, showing the military-style clothing for schoolboys that was worn throughout the twentieth century.

**LEFT:** A box of colored pencils from the Horobasha Pencil Factory.

**BELOW:** Tiny children's magazines arrive in the "Library Bus."

**A writing tablet, entitled "Science,"
which also urges support for the Olympics.**

RIGHT: Label on a package of the Light of Peace sparklers.

LEFT: "Big and Strong" says the umbrella of a boy samurai on this *uchiwa*, or summer fan.

161

ABOVE: A package
of Boy brand caramel candy.

LEFT: A package of "Sunday Chewing-
Gam," and a collection of milk caramel
packages, including one with a scene of
children playing tortoise and hare.

A Japanese syllabary card game in which letters, shown on these cards, are matched with stories on other cards.

Two updated versions of a traditional game called Shogi with wooden tokens played like chess: **Great Armed Forces**, 1940s, top, and **New Army Rocket**, 1950s, bottom and right.

二人で遊べる。
し駒は計五箇
その内訳は左記
（１）大将

| | | |
|---|---|---|
| 中将（１） | 少将 |
| 大佐（１） | 中佐 |
| 大尉（１） | 中尉（１） |
| 原子爆弾（１） | |
| ヒコーキ（１） | |

スパイ別に列挙した駒
残余各々を少々

◆配置方法
立合向て十五を裏に
若くは駒を突合せる
相手の駒と勝負は宜し

◆入れは
勝する。

◆各駒の勢力
◎大将以元
○ＭＰは少尉まで
◎ヒコーキは原子爆弾に
◎ＭＰはスパイに
○スパイは其他に
ＭＰに負け其他に勝つ
原子爆弾は他に勝並
他に勝
其他に負

◆注意
敵の区域内に
は必ず交戦に
は敵出大の処に
中央丸より
左右何れより
出される

**A** paper party mask,
which was exported and
sold in the United States in
the 1950s for 12 cents.

A sheet of temporary tattoos, showing Western and Japanese characters.

NEXT PAGE: A child's paradise of cheap and ingenious toys flooded American five-and-dime stores in the years immediately after World War II.

"Change their clothes" state these two sheets of paper
dolls, one of a father and son and one of a little girl.

昭和44年8月1日発行（毎月1回1日発行）第8巻第5号　昭和38年1月8日第3種郵便物認可

# よいこの がくしゅう

とくしゅう たろうごう つきへ いく

8

ABOVE: A futuristic toy car.

BELOW: A space fish, by the Yoshiya toy makers, 1950s.

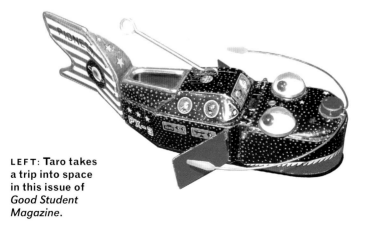

LEFT: Taro takes a trip into space in this issue of *Good Student Magazine*.

おもちゃ お買物あそび

ひこうき
2.200えん

きんぎょ
100えん

ミキサー
3.700えん

ままごと
どうぐ
400えん

日本人形
5.300 えん

消防
自動
車
3.500えん

ふらんす人形
2.500えん

まり
100えん

松盛堂

HOUSE
700

Children could cut out the merchandise, cut out the money, and play the Toy Shopping Game.

177

**LEFT:** This kite has an image of a boy riding on a good-luck carp.

**RIGHT:** The face on this kite is a traditional Kabuki character of a crazed woman, meant to ward off evil spirits.

女べらほう

Japanese domestic life is turned into a board game advertising the

National brand of products of the Matsushita Electric Industry.

These circular cards, called *menko*, can be used as sports cards or to play various types of games.

RIGHT: Up to bat is Nishizawa of the Dragons, pitching is Fujimoto of the Giants, and at the bottom is Kaneda of the Tigers.

BELOW: These cards illustrate the fastball, the steal, and the home run, and can be used to play a Japanese version of paper-rock-scissors called *janken*.

巨人（ジアンツ）　藤本

中日（ドラゴンズ）　西澤

600

1500

阪神（タイガース）　金田

Tiger

183

184

Two issues of *Baseball Magazine* from 1971, featuring the Yomiuri Giants, left, and Kazuo Kageyama of the Nankai Hawks, below.

LEFT: These game cards demonstrate baseball players' positions, including "strong pitcher," "heavy hitter," and "catcher."

増巳山（三保ヶ関）35才　佐久昇（立浪）27才　佐賀ノ里（二所ノ関）23才　平鹿川（立
6尺　26貫和歌山県出身　5.7尺 25貫長野県出身　6尺　27貫　佐賀県出身　5.9尺 26貫秋

松錦（中村）28才　七ツ海（立浪）29才　佐賀光（二所ノ関）23才　大田山（高
5.7尺 23貫北海道出身　6.2尺 29貫茨城県出身　5.8尺 24貫佐賀県出身　5.8尺 32貫東

186

This pamphlet, an insert in the magazine *Sumo* for May 15, 1958, contains a photo roster of sumo wrestlers of the period.

波（立浪）34才　前ケ潮（高砂）26才　羽子錦（高島）21才　出羽湊（出羽ノ海）34才
30貫石川県出身 5.8尺 24貫岐阜県出身 5.9尺 36貫兵庫県出身 5.9尺 26貫青森県出身

山（荒磯）31才　天津灘（二所ノ関）26才　東海（荒磯）33才　福乃里（吉葉山）32才
29貫秋田県出身 5.9尺 28貫佐賀県出身 5.8尺 42貫東京都出身 5.8尺 22貫福岡県出身

十両全力士写真名鑑

Sumo wrestling stars on die-cut *menko* cards.

決戦

**LEFT:**
A flyer for a judo match announcing the "decisive battle."

**RIGHT:**
A sports card showing the sumo wrestler Toki Tsu Yama.

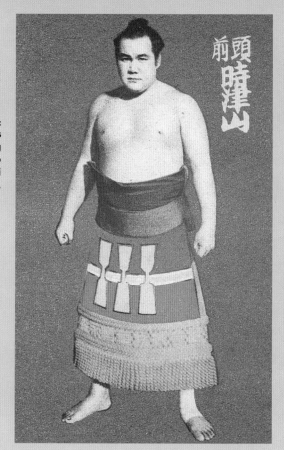

前頭 時津山

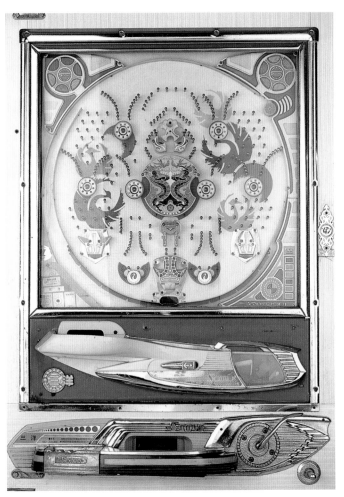

Pachinko is a pinball-like game that's part skill but mostly luck.
These space-age designs are from the 1960s, which was

the end of the era of hand-assembled machines. The machine
above was made by Nishijin, the one on the left by Sanyo.

A style of folk music called *minyo* and a soulful ballad pop style later called *enka* dominated music in the postwar years. This collection includes records by Haruo Minami, who was one of the most popular traditional singers in both genres.

みんなラジオをききましょう

ABOVE: A 45-rpm record sleeve, featuring
the many singing stars of **RCA** Victor Japan.

LEFT: "Everybody, let's listen to radio"
announces this poster featuring women
voices of the **NHK**, or Japanese
**B**roadcasting **C**orporation's public radio.

**ABOVE:** A poster for the movie *Spell of the Sand Drawing*, 1960, "the long-awaited samurai drama" in which the mystery of a dying shogun's wishes are finally revealed.

**LEFT:** A poster for the movie *Nagurikomi Songoku*, a version of the famous Chinese tale of the Monkey King, from Daiei Films.

RIGHT: A poster for the movie *Bloody Duel*, "The famous modern fight story," asks "What will the outcome be for the champion of the century and the inexperienced challenger?" Made by Daiei Films.

佐田啓

THIS PAGE: Popular movie stars Kenji Sada, above, and Yoshiko Kuga, right, are featured on these cards, which were gift inserts in an entertainment magazine.

久我美子　明星四月号附録

These two posters announce special showings of silent-era movies. The one above is for *Chushingura*, a famous historical drama screened in memory of its star, Tsumasaburo Bando; to the right is *Vortex of Revenge*, screened as a tribute to the pioneer director of early Japanese movies, Shozo Makino.

# 明治百年記念興行

毎日テレビでお馴染みカツドウ屋一代男に活躍する
目玉の松ちゃんこと尾上松之助をはじめ映画界の
王者をしめる俳優たちを育てたマキノ省三！
豪華キャストで綴る　超大作！
無聲映画の醍醐味！！

日本映画育ての親マキノ省三氏を偲ぶ活動大寫眞

## 復讐の渦巻

ソ満国境を越えソ聯に生きる
日本一の美人女優
万年娘とたたえられた
梨園より
貫録充分
御存知長谷川一夫
今は昔偲ぶ名優

岡田嘉子
森静子
坂東好太郎
市川右太衛門
林長二郎
阪東妻三郎

カツベン
辨士・太鼓・三味線・ペット
楽団舞台で演奏する葵楽団一行

辨界の横綱

声色
徳川一郎
泉宏東
伍光郎

**The 10th International Sports Movie Award went to this documentary called *The Story of Yoshio Shirai*, about a boxer who thrilled Japan by becoming a world champion.**

The movie *Record of Blood* documents the World
Professional Wrestling League Games and includes the
Japanese champ Rikidosan, top right circle.

ABOVE: The movie *Onna Sazan*, or "Woman Sazan Warrior," was made in the late 1940s by Shintoho Studios, which specialized at the time in artistically ambitious productions.

RIGHT: The movie *Rashomon*, 1950, helped establish Japanese movies as fine art in the West and made the director Akira Kurosawa and the actor Toshiro Mifune international stars.

ABOVE: A poster for *Pond of the Seven Vengeful Spirits*, a story of "gruesome horror and fear . . . bizarre love and lust," which announces its "summer evening show," a popular time for scary movies.

RIGHT: This 1961 religious epic, *Shaka* ("Buddha"), was "The large-scale drama of the century," a movie of "miracles and romance." It was directed by Kenji Misumi, with special effects by Tatsuyuki Yokota, for Daiei Films.

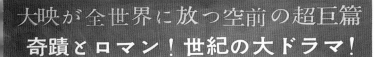

# 大映が全世界に放つ空前の超巨篇
## 奇蹟とロマン！世紀の大ドラマ！

製作 永田雅一

総天然色

# 釈迦
しゃか

島田竜三　丹羽又三郎　三田村元　阿井美ひろ　<!-- 以下キャスト名縦書き、判読困難 -->

細川ちか子　北林谷栄　月丘夢路　山田五十鈴

大映超特作

LEFT:
Complex
moods and
noir themes
characterize
postwar films
in these
publicity stills
from movies
of the 1950s.

RIGHT:
Handbills
of movies
playing at the
Silver Star
Hall, in the
town of Iida,
Nagano
Prefecture,
1959.

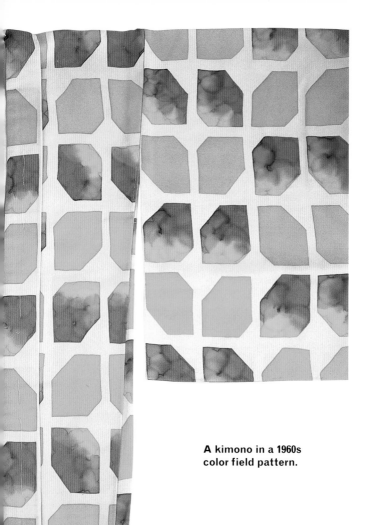

**A** kimono in a 1960s color field pattern.

A kimono in a 1960s
op art pattern.

海へも
おいしい
サンヨーの缶詰を

SUNYO BRAND

サンヨー子

1

**ABOVE:** An ad for Sunyo brand canned food says "Delicious – bring it to the seaside too."

**RIGHT:** A carton of cigarettes makes a great summertime gift, according to this ad from the Japan Tobacco Company.

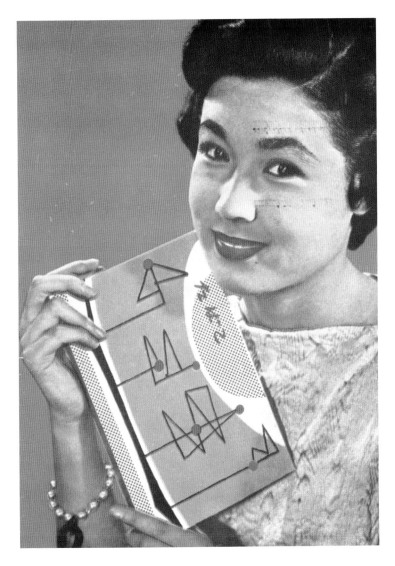

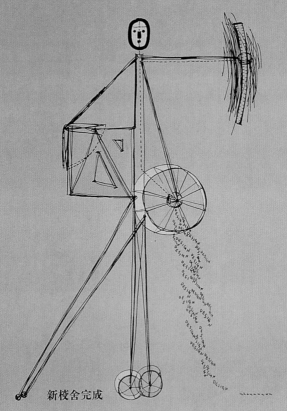

新校舎完成

伊東茂平先生講座　毎月開講・イトウ式新立体製圖

# カロン洋裁・生徒募集

本科・別科〔夜間〕・日曜科★受付９月１日→３０日

財團法人・所長　國松惠美子・大阪御堂筋大丸南西向イ（守田ビル）

LEFT: "Students wanted to learn new techniques in pattern making," says this poster for Karon Dressmaking School from 1951.

RIGHT: This poster for Penigin Women's Medicine, made by the Sankyo Company, is in a long, narrow format similar to a traditional scroll.

一回ですっきり

こしけの薬 ペニギン

SANKYO 三共

3錠入・10錠入

三共株式会社

Issues **10** and **11** of *Hana,* or "The Flower," a journal
of modern flower arranging, which was published
by **Seika Nishizaka** in **Kyoto** in the 1950s.

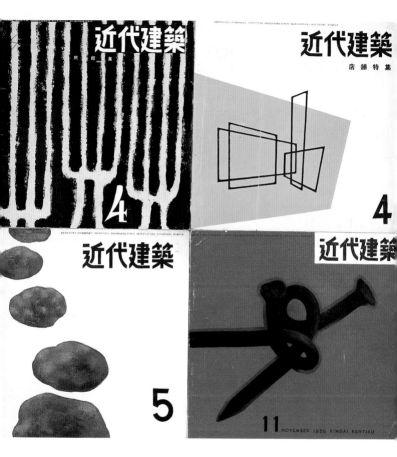

Four modernist covers of the architecture
trade magazine *Kindai Kentiku,* from 1956.

ABOVE: A road map distributed by Japan Air Lines, featuring a car called the Toyopet Crown Deluxe on the back cover.

RIGHT: A fan given away in the 1960s at Tokyo International Airport (now Haneda Airport) for "enjoyment of cool summer evenings."

東京国際空港

TOKYO INTERNATIONAL AIRPORT

納涼夜間開場
7月10日 8月末日

223

Two souvenir cigarette
packages from Expo '70, Osaka,
Japan's first world's fair.

皆様の **富士銀行**

The 1960s logo of Fuji Bank,
on a matchbox cover.

FURNITURE
KUBO
(保)

株式
会社 久保商店

ABOVE: **A catalog from the Kubo Furniture Company, featuring their Kureharon line of folding tables and chairs.**

RIGHT: **A bamboo and paper fan from the 1960s.**

227

≪ステレオ≫ PERFECT SOUND 6

# ガール・フレンド

オックス　　花の指環（ゆび・わ）

VICTOR
VP-8

奥村真利

Polydor
SDP-2011

MONA LIZA'S SMILE

# モナ・リザの微笑

STEREO
¥37

ザ・タイガース
真赤なジャケット
RED JACKET

THE TIGERS

Polydor Records

THE TIGERS

AK-531
(SAS-631)

ステレオ

45
rpm

¥600

恋慕かんざし

歌謡舞踊シリーズ　B面振りつき

東映映画「小判鮫・お役者仁義」主題歌

美空ひばり

お役者仁義

東映映画「小判鮫・お役者仁義」主題歌

HIBARI MISORA

**ABOVE:** A 45-rpm recording of "Love and a Hairpin," a theme song
from the movie *The Chivalry, Benevolence and Righteousness
of a Kabuki Actor*, sung by the actress Hibari Misora.
Here she is seeking vengeance for her Kabuki actor lover.

**LEFT:** The 45-rpm record covers for Oksudu and their
song "The Girlfriend," above, and the Tigers and
their hit single "Mona Liza's Smile," bottom.

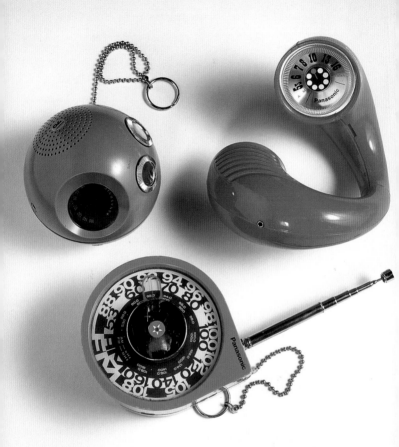

Panasonic explored playful shapes in portable radios in the
early 1970s with its Panapet ball-shaped radio (green), the
Toot-a-Loop radio intended to be worn as a bracelet (red),
and the Rolling Tone AM/FM radio (blue).

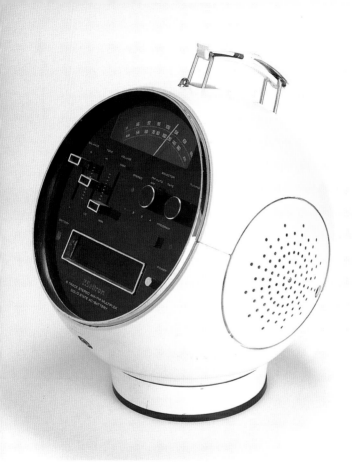

The side grill speakers enhance the suggestion
of a space helmet on this **Weltron model 2001 AM/FM**
radio and 8-track player, 1970.

The baseball hero Hyuma Hoshi of the comic book series "Star of the Giants" appears on these chopsticks meant for school lunchboxes. He was a fictional boy–pitcher for a real team: the Yomiuri Giants.

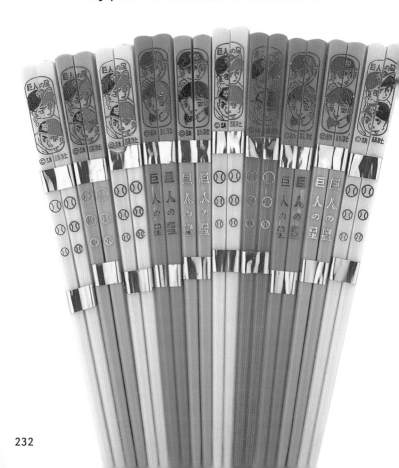

**G**ame cards of the characters in the **P**aaman
comics series, adventures of a grade school boy turned
superhero, which began in **1966**.

Above is a cover of the record album
*Ultimate Edition! All About Ultraman!* On the
back cover, right, the legendary Ultraman,
who was created in 1966, is in the center,
flanked by members of his Ultra family,
including Ultra Seven, Ultraman A, Ultraman
Taro, and Ultraman Leo. Song titles include
"Song of the Giant Monster," "Ultra March,"
"Song of Ultra Boy," "Ballad of Ultra
Mother," "Fight! Ultra Leo," and "Ballad
of the Starry Sky." The album is by
King Records, 1979.

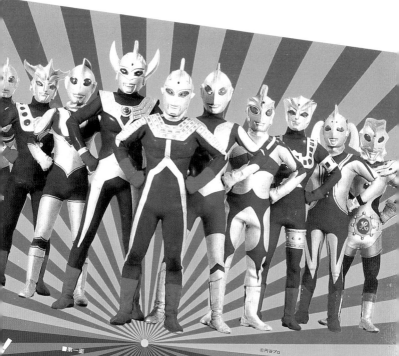

©円谷プロ

RECORD CO.,LTD 発売元・キングレコード株式会社 レコードから無断で複製その他に録音することは法律で禁じられています

名場面他のカラー70点以上をちりばめた
豪華写真集ジャケット

**Rockbat, the catlike hero with chest wheels, is a toy based on a live-action television show from the early 1970s.**

An action figure called Yunkers F2, an adversary of Mach Baron, from a 1970s TV series.

237

**Action scenes on post-cards from the early 1970s television show** *Kamen Rider*.

**Monsters and heroes are featured on these *menko* cards from the 1970s.**

241

In the early 1980s, when the evil Warader Empire invaded Earth, a toy manufacturer named Takara evolved a robot that could transform from its disguise as a car or an airplane into a fighting machine/warrior. Thus Transformers were born. In Japan the hit TV show proclaimed "Fight! Super Robot Lifeform Transformers!" By the mid-1980s Transformers were popular worldwide.

"Find the right arm! Find the left arm! Who can complete the robot first?" asks a board game based on a TV show about the robot hero Mazinger Z. This game is made by Popy, a company specializing in toys related to comic and animated characters.

**Vampire Bat Man**, one of the
enemies of Kamen Rider,
appears on a calendar for 1972.

**A coin purse featuring Kamen Rider, the
comic book and animation hero developed
by the famous cartoonist Shotaro Ishimori.**

イナズマン

© 石森プロ・NETテレビ・東映

**A** fan featuring the character Inazuman and his extraordinary car, from the **TV** series by Toei Studios, 1975.

247

**The Message from Space** *bento* **box
for children's lunches, with a divider for
rice and a little soy sauce bottle.**

**A** thermos with shoulder strap and **ID** tag
featuring characters from the **TV** show
*Ninja Kyaptor*. **The** characters' face masks
represent symbols of the elements.

**A children's mask of the character
Kitaro from the cartoon series**
*Ge Ge Ge No Kitaro*.

**Assembly is required for this model of a strange female ghost called Rokuro Kubi, from the Crown Model Monster Series No. 2.**

**A modern fan shaped like an insect wing.**

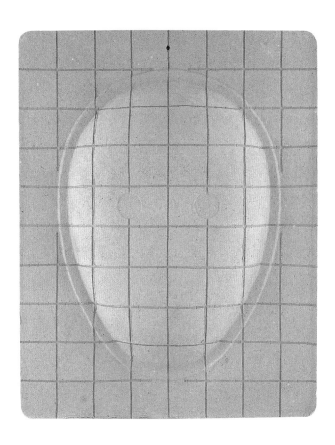

A mold for use in a crafts project
from **Tokyu Hands**, a popular
arts and crafts supply store.

# Credits

Pages 15, 75, 109, 179, 242: From the collection of Moto Hyun

Pages 18, 48, 221: From the collection of Nick Carter

Pages 19, 51, 59, 82, 94, 170, 172, 191, 195: From the collection of Kalim Winata

Pages 80, 81: Permission courtesy of the Shiseido Corporate Museum

Pages 23, 91, 92, 122, 130, 136, 137, 180, 207, 218: Copyright by Yoshida Hideo Memorial Foundation, Advertising Museum Tokyo

Pages 24, 73, 216, 217: Tobacco and Salt Museum, Tokyo

Pages 64, 65, 66, 67, 114, 115: Copyright by the Ohara Institute for Social Research, Hosei University, Tokyo


Most photography by Alan Borrud Photography, Portland, Oregon. Additional photography by Reed Darmon.

Translations by Tom Conrad and Junko Igarashi, Port Angeles, Washington, and Kay Inoue, Portland, Oregon.

# Acknowledgments

As always, thanks to Kalim Winata, longtime friend and collaborator, for the use of many images and for his cultural input. And thanks also to Moto Hyun for several items from his "lifetime accumulation" and for his travel companionship.

Thanks to Steve Mockus at Chronicle Books for his critical insights and his trust.

For the generous use of his vast collection, I would like to thank Japanese ephemera and postcard dealer Yoji Kan, Bellevue, Washington. And I am especially grateful to Billy Galaxy of Portland, Oregon, who, with his keen eye for pop culture, brought back many treasures from his Japanese shopping expeditions.

Special thanks go to Tom Conrad and Junko Igarashi for their skilled research and expert translations and to Kay Inoue for additional translations.

I am very grateful to Hiroko Ozeki at Shiseido, New York, and to Yoshifumi Shizume at the Tobacco and Salt Museum, Tokyo. I am especially grateful to Noriko Iwamoto at the Advertising Museum Tokyo for his help and patience in granting access to their extraordinary collection.

モダン
室町の陶酔郷

電日本橋 I078